FLIGHT

*How to Get
the Job That
Launches Your
Career After
College*

PATH

NEIL C. KALT, PH.D., AND
WILLIAM B. HELMREICH, PH.D.

A FIRESIDE BOOK
Published by SIMON & SCHUSTER INC.
New York   London   Toronto   Sydney   Tokyo

Fireside
Simon & Schuster Building
Rockefeller Center
1230 Avenue of the Americas
New York, New York 10020

FIRESIDE and colophon are registered trademarks
of Simon & Schuster Inc.

Designed by Levavi and Levavi
Manufactured in the United States of America

10 9 8 7 6 5 4 3 2 1

Library of Congress Cataloging in Publication Data

Kalt, Neil C.
  Flight Path.

  "A Fireside book."
  Bibliography: p.
  1. Job hunting—United States.   2. College graduates—
Employment—United States.   3. Vocational guidance—United
States.   I. Helmreich, William B.   II. Title.
HF5382.75.U6K35   1989   650.1'4   88–34926
ISBN 0-671-67286-X

For all the young men and women who face the challenge of making the leap from the classroom to the world of work. This book's for you.

TABLE OF CONTENTS

INTRODUCTION

So You Want a Job . . .

Today's job market is jam-packed with applicants, and the competition for good jobs is fierce. That's why it's so important to know how to get a job you want—how to *make it happen*. This book tells you how: how to find out what kinds of jobs are right for you; how to put together a resume that'll make people want to meet you; how to find out where the jobs are; how to get interviews; how to get ready for each interview; how to make the strongest possible case for your candidacy when you are interviewed; how to follow up; and how to decide if the job and the company are right for you.

This isn't the first book of its kind; nor will it be the last. It is, however, the most usable. Intentionally short, it's organized and presented in a way that makes it easy to read and understand, and it's packed with information you can put your hands on and use. In short, it gives you the tools you need to compete, to become a persuasive advocate of your candidacy, to get the kind of job you want.

A Note About Gender

The world of work has clearly become, at virtually all levels, a place of opportunity for women as well as men. As a result, you're going to be interviewed by men and by women in your quest for a job. And that's as it should be. Unfortunately, this presented us with a dilemma; namely, how to refer to the interviewer. We had two choices. We could use "he" at some times and "she" at others, which would be accurate though awkward, or we could limit ourselves to the traditional "he," which would give the book consistency and be easier for the reader to follow. Feeling that ease of reading was more important than the accuracy of the interviewer's gender, we chose the traditional "he." As you read the book, we think you'll find that this choice makes sense.

FLIGHT
PATH

CHAPTER ONE

How to Decide What Kind of Job You Want

When you start thinking about a job, there's only one good place to begin: decide what kind of job you want. The work you choose should interest you, make good use of your skills and abilities, and give you opportunities to learn and grow. Some jobs will meet these requirements. A lot more won't, which is why it's so important to begin by investing care and effort in deciding what kind of work you want to do.

Faced with thousands of different jobs, how do you narrow the field to a manageable few? By taking a hard look at your education, work experience, skills, likes, dislikes, and aspirations, then deciding in which directions they point. Direction is the key. It may be obvious. It may be hard to find. But it's there. To help you find it, let's look at the things that'll point you toward certain kinds of jobs and away from others, that'll give you the sense of yourself which you need to begin evaluating different kinds of work and deciding which ones are right for you.

SOURCES OF DIRECTION

Direction lies in your answers to the following questions:

What Are You Good At? What Skills Do You Have?

- Are you good with people? Are you persuasive? Articulate? Are you a leader?
- Are you good at organizing things? At managing projects? At getting things done?
- Do you like helping others? Dealing with their problems? Helping to solve them?
- Do you enjoy gathering information? Do you like work that requires attention to detail?
- Do you like work that's physical? Are you good at working with your hands?
- Are you good at problem solving, at identifying problems and finding solutions?
- Are you creative? Artistic? Innovative? Good at generating ideas?

What Kind of Education Do You Have?

From the vantage point of someone who's looking for a job, major fields of study range from those that are sharply focused—such as accounting, nursing, and engineering—to those that are more abstract—fields such as history and philosophy. If your training is sharply focused and points to an area in which you are interested, direction isn't a problem. You know where you're headed. Even if you have a last-minute change of heart and want to do something else, you'll probably be able to apply the skills you've acquired in a number of other fields. So don't discount them.

If you majored in a field like marketing, finance, or communications, you're suited for jobs in all kinds of industries. For example, people with degrees in marketing work for manufacturers of cosmetics, detergents, and canned soups; for computer companies, banks, and airlines; and for credit-card companies, television networks, and professional sports organizations. So it's not a matter of options. There are lots of them. It's a matter of which industries interest you and are most likely to give you a chance to grow.

Even if school was a labor of love and you chose a major that wasn't directly applicable to the job market—like history, philosophy, or English literature—don't feel that your chances of getting a good job are about the same as your chances of winning the lottery. You've been taught to think, to write clearly, and to learn, skills that *count* in the business world. Look for work and for companies where they're valued.

What Kinds of Jobs Have You Held?

"Experience" is one of the magic words, enhancing your status and increasing your value. If you've held a job in a given field—a part-time job with an accounting firm, a summer job with an advertising agency—you have an inside track on another job in the same field.

Even if you haven't had a "status-enhancing" job, skills you acquired and things you learned about yourself from ordinary jobs can point to—or away from—different kinds of work.

What Other Things Have You Done that Might Give You Direction?

- An internship in the mayor's office could lead to a job as an administrative assistant to a state senator or county executive.
- Editing your college newspaper might be the key to a job in publishing.
- Volunteer work at a community service center may whet your interest in a full-time job in social work.
- Filming weddings and confirmations for friends and relatives might be the experience you need for an entry-level job in video or film production.

- Skills acquired at home on a personal computer could help you get a job as a programmer.

Which Aspects of Work Appeal to You? Which Aspects Do You Dislike?

- Do you want a desk job or would you rather be up and around?
- How much job-related traveling do you want to do?
- How much time do you want to spend working alone? How much do you want to spend working with others?
- Do you prefer work that's fast paced or unhurried?
- How much money do you want to make—now and in the future?

Taken together, the answers to these questions should give you a fairly well defined sense of what you like, what you don't like, and what you have to offer. Use this profile to get a handle on the kinds of work that are right for you. Start by identifying the kinds of jobs that are likely to fit your particular mix of skills, preferences, and training. Later, use this sense of yourself to evaluate the jobs you interview for.

FINDING OUT WHAT KINDS OF JOBS ARE RIGHT FOR YOU

Two of the best places to start your search are the *Encyclopedia of Careers and Vocational Guidance* and the *Occupational Outlook Handbook*. The encyclopedia consists of three volumes: focus on the first two. The first describes in considerable detail the kinds of work people do and the career opportunities in a broad range of fields: for example, aerospace manufacturing, the automobile industry, federal government service, foreign trade, insurance, magazine publishing, the printing industry, recreation, and real estate. The second volume looks at more than 200 occupations, though the ones you're most likely to care about are the 101 that are labeled professional, administrative, and managerial. Information about each occupation includes a definition; a brief history; a fairly detailed overview of the nature of the work; working conditions; the training and certification, if any, that are required; the skills, preferences, and personality traits that seem to enable people in each occupation to like what they're doing and to do it well; methods of getting into the occupation; advancing in the occupation; earnings; employment outlook; and sources of additional information.

The *Occupational Outlook Handbook*, like the second volume of the *Encyclopedia of Careers and Vocational Guidance*, contains information about nearly 250 occupations. In addition to most of the areas that the encyclopedia covers, the handbook also looks at the kinds of companies that hire people in each occupation. Given your background, skills, and occupational interests, the handbook's scope is also likely to be broader than the encyclopedia's. To give you a sense of the ground that the handbook covers, we've listed the occupational categories that are likely to interest most college graduates:

- Managerial and management-related occupations
- Engineers, surveyors, and architects
- Natural, computer, and mathematical scientists
- Lawyers, social scientists, social workers, and religious workers
- Teachers, librarians, and counselors
- Health diagnosing and treating practitioners
- Registered nurses, pharmacists, dietitians, therapists, and physician assistants
- Health technologists and technicians
- Technologists and technicians, except health
- Marketing and sales occupations
- Service occupations
- Agriculture, forestry, fishing, and related occupations
- Job opportunities in the armed forces

Besides the traditional or mainstream occupations, both the encyclopedia and the handbook look at a mix of less-than-typical careers. For example, the encyclopedia covers actors and actresses, air traffic controllers, city managers, dancers, fashion designers, foreign service officers, funeral directors, models, careers in music, radio and television announcers, state police officers, urban planners, and writers. Similarly, the handbook looks at actors, chefs, choreographers, corrections officers, dancers, designers, directors, musicians, and pilots. The encyclopedia and the handbook can be found in the reference section of any good library.

After you've spent some time with the *Occupational Outlook Handbook* and the *Encyclopedia of Careers and Vocational Guidance*, try the Office of Career Counseling and Placement at your college or university. Normally, you'll find people who've been trained to help you discover what kinds of jobs are right for you. Use them—they can make a real difference.

At this point, you should have a pretty fair sense of the kinds of work you would and wouldn't like to do. Try to add to what you've learned by using a third source of information: people who work in the fields that interest you. Contact the ones you know first—just pick up the phone, tell them you're trying to find out as much as you can about their fields, then ask if they'll spend a little time telling you about the things they do. Chances are, they'll be happy to.

It'll take more time and effort to arrange meetings with the people you don't know, but it's worth the effort. These people can tell you a lot. Start with a good library and find out which directories carry the names of people who work in the fields that interest you. Then compile a list of names, companies, addresses, and phone numbers. Sometimes your college's career placement center will offer a service that can put you in touch with school alumni who work in the fields in which you're interested. Make sure you make use of all avenues open to you in looking for a position for which you are well suited. Write a brief letter to about six people in each field, telling them you want to learn more about their fields and professions and that you'll call shortly for an appointment. Then call. If your letters are well written and you're polite and well spoken on the phone, you should have no trouble getting a number of appointments. When you do, prepare carefully for each one. Think about the questions you want to ask. Know what you want to find out. Then do it.

By this time, you should have a fairly well defined sense of the kinds of jobs that are right for you. Given this sense of direction, you're ready to start working on your resume.

CHAPTER TWO

How to Put Together a Resume

Most people seem to feel that putting together a resume is like taking medicine: unpleasant but necessary. Many people would even argue that "frustrating" and "painful" come closer to the mark. Why? Because you're being asked to write a compelling one-page sales piece, with you as the merchandise. If you're Phi Beta Kappa, editor of the school newspaper, a member of the debating and track teams, and you've held a number of interesting, challenging part-time and summer jobs, putting together your resume is something you probably look forward to. However, if your accomplishments are somewhat more typical, preparing a resume can be scary. After all, the companies you send it to only know what that piece of paper tells them. Until you're interviewed, you *are* the information and impressions that your resume conveys.

Your resume has one goal: to get you interviews. Unfortunately, the people who'll see your resume will also see lots of others. So yours has to be as good as it can. It has to make the strongest possible case for your candidacy by creating an image that will make people want to meet you. There are many ways to put together a resume that will achieve these objectives, but no easy, cut-and-dried formula to get you there. However, the right guidelines can take you a good part of the way. The rest depends on you—the things you've done; your ability to describe them clearly, briefly, and impressively; and your willingness to make the effort that preparing a first-rate resume requires.

GENERAL CONSIDERATIONS

1. The people who see your resume will spend less than one minute taking a first—and possibly last—look at it. To stand out from the rest, it must be organized, written, and designed in a way that makes it easy to read, emphasizes the most important things you've done, and makes the reader feel you're special.

2. Write your own resume if you can. It'll help get you ready for interviews by forcing you to decide what you do and don't want potential employers to know about you, and by making you write about the things you've done as clearly, briefly, and favorably as you can. If you use a resume-writing service, there's a good chance that the people who see your resume will know it and that may hurt you. Why? Because resumes prepared by professional services don't always look and sound like the work of newly minted college graduates. If the people who read your resume feel that you didn't write it, they're likely to conclude that you don't have much faith in yourself. They're also likely to have doubts about your ability to organize information, doubts about your ability to write, and doubts about whether your resume accurately describes your activities and jobs you've held.

   Are there any circumstances under which you should use a resume-writing service? There sure are. Let's say you've tried to write your resume. Several times. You've shown the latest draft to friends and family, and nobody likes it very much—especially you. Your resume just doesn't look good, it doesn't read well, and it doesn't begin to do you justice. You need help. Badly. A resume-writing service is probably the best place to get it, despite the cost. If the resume they write isn't too slick and doesn't contain too many words that you wouldn't use, you'll come away with a resume that'll work.

3. Whatever you have to say about yourself, say it in one page. If you must use more than one page, have very good reasons for doing so. Because if the first page isn't particularly impressive, the chances are excellent that prospective employers won't want to see the second.

4. Writing a first-rate resume takes time, effort, more time, and more effort. So plan to write several drafts before you're done. When you've completed each draft, set it aside for a day or two, then read it carefully and revise it as needed.

5. Always lead with your strongest suit. The most important sections of your resume will probably be your education and your work experience. Start your resume with the one that's more likely to impress potential employers. It'll increase your chances of creating a favorable impression, getting people to keep reading, and making them want to look more closely at the things you've said and done.

6. Limit yourself to the things you've done well. Your resume is not a candid list of your strengths and weaknesses, the good and the bad choices you've made. It's a sales pitch, and while it should be factual, it should also be carefully selective. The only information in it should be information that makes you attractive and strengthens your candidacy. It should never contain anything that doesn't.

7. Write sentences that are brief, clear, and informative. Short sentences are easier to read, follow, and understand than long ones. They can also create a more favorable impression: three or four short sentences taken together

can suggest that you've done more than one or two long ones, even though both sets of sentences contain the same information.

Whether short or long, every sentence must be clearly written. The person reading your resume should be able to process the information in each sentence quickly and easily. Businesses want people who can communicate clearly, and they'll keep looking till they find them.

Each sentence gives you a chance to tell potential employers more about yourself, to flesh out and strengthen the image you're trying to create. So make each sentence count. Make it informative. And use it to tell the person who reads it something about you that he hasn't already learned.

8. Use the *past tense* to describe your work experience and extracurricular activities. Remember, you're writing about things you've already done. Exceptions are activities you're doing now and a job you currently hold, which you should describe in the present tense.

9. Don't use the word "I" to begin sentences that describe things you've done. Instead, begin with words that convey action: *created, formed, initiated, developed, assisted, directed, designed, collaborated, implemented, advised, supervised, established, assembled, organized, prepared, conducted, and evaluated.*

10. No matter how well written, organized, and presented you feel your resume is, get at least one person whose judgment about written material you respect to critique it. Someone who's good will almost always have suggestions that will make your resume better.

11. Don't send out a resume that isn't spotless—no smudges, no erasures, no typos, no visible corrections. And make sure your grammar, spelling, and punctuation are on the mark. They're a first hurdle, and if you fail to take it cleanly, there's a chance that you'll take yourself out of contention no matter what else your resume says.

THE CONTENT OF YOUR RESUME

There are two kinds of information that your resume must contain—information about your education and information about your work experience. After that, you're free to use whatever categories best capture the substance and spirit of the things you've done—coursework, extracurricular activities, honors, skills, publications, professional organizations, and interests.

Let's take a look at each of the sections that are likely to appear on a resume:

Identifying Information

Your name, address, and phone number head your resume. If you're sending out resumes while you're still in school and your school address and home address are different, include both—and accompanying phone numbers—on your resume.

Objective

If you decide to include it, your objective would be stated in a single sentence and would describe the type of position you want. There are two ways to do this. You can describe a position in a particular field. For example:

"A marketing position with a major manufacturer of packaged goods."

"To work in the news department of a radio or television station."

"A position as a designer in a children's clothing company."

Or you can tie your skills and abilities to a position in a particular field. For example:

"To apply skills in research design, data analysis, and report writing in a marketing research position."

"A position in the managerial structure of a major department store. Seek to use knowledge of organizations, of people, and of retailing."

"To use social-service training and administrative skills as an administrator in a nonprofit organization."

Your objective is something you can include or omit. Should you include it? If the position you describe is the only one you want and you'd reject an offer to take any other position, include your objective on your resume. However, if there are other positions you'd consider and you'd like to keep your options open, leave it out. Moreover, if you apply for more than one type of job and you state your objective on your resume, you're going to need a different resume for each type of job. So save your objective for cover letters and interviews in which you don't have to restrict yourself to one or two sentences and you can tailor your objective to the specific needs of each job and company.

Education

The first major selling point on your resume is your college education. Most of you just spent four years taking courses, getting grades, and earning a degree. Now you have a chance to make that work for you.

Include the following information in this section:

- The name of the school that granted your degree. If you attended more than one school or have more than one degree, start with the school you attended most recently, then work your way back.
- The city or town and state in which each school is located.
- The degree you will be or have been granted. Abbreviate your degree—B.A., B.S., B.B.A., or B.F.A.—unless

there's a chance that potential employers won't know what the letters stand for.

- The year your degree will be or was awarded. Use the year you expect your degree to be granted even if you haven't graduated yet. Potential employers will understand, and it'll save you the trouble of having another resume typed and copied after you graduate.
- Your major and minor areas of study.
- Your overall grade point average and/or major grade point average, if you feel they're high enough to be mentioned.
- Any honors or awards you received—scholarships, dean's list, graduating magna cum laude, honor societies, and departmental awards. If you list an award, indicate what it means: for example, "the Clark Award, given to the graduating senior with the highest average in accounting," or "the MacDowell Award, given for service to the University."
- Any professional or trade association seminars you've attended.

If you worked to help pay for part or all of your education, say so. This says a number of things about you, all of them good—that you're mature, determined, and responsible. Use a sentence at the end of this section to get this information across. For example, "Worked to pay for 50% of college costs." Or, "Financed 75% of college costs by working."

Experience

A description of the jobs you've held is the second major selling point of your resume. Which is why you'll probably regard your work experience as a real stumbling block. Don't. The vast majority of college students who've worked have done so in work-study programs, part-time jobs, and/or summer jobs. Sure, work that's related to the kinds of jobs you're applying for is clearly a plus. But so is having worked at all. A record of employment shows that you want to work, you're able to find work, and you can hold a job.

A description of each job you've held should include the following:

- The name and address of the company or institution you worked for.
- The title of the job you held.
- The month and year you started and the month and year you left.
- The things you did. Don't feel compelled to list everything; instead, focus on the things that were most important and required the kinds of skills and abilities you're trying to market now. Describe them briefly and clearly. Don't make up accomplishments. You don't have to. Nobody expects an undergraduate to hold jobs of great scope and responsibility. Nobody expects singular achievements. If you've held several jobs, one or two that were interesting and challenging, and you did some good work, you're ahead of the game.

Ordinarily, you'd describe your most recent job first, then work backward. If you held increasingly important jobs, listing them chronologically is the best way to make that clear. However, if you've held several jobs that are related to the kind of position you're applying for and several jobs that are not, forget about listing them chronologically. Instead, create appropriate subheadings, group your jobs accordingly, then list them chronologically. For example, under the subheading "Marketing Research," list the summer job you had as a research assistant at a marketing research company and the part-time work you did as a research assistant in your college's marketing department. The summer jobs you held as a lifeguard and waiter would go under a different subheading, something like "Resort Work." Using these subheadings puts the two research jobs together, sets them apart, gets them up front, and enables them to have the impact they should.

Should you list all the jobs you've held, however short-term, pedestrian, and unrelated to the kind of work you want to do now? If you've held no more than three jobs, list them all. At the very least they indicate that you have a record of employment and that you've looked for, gotten, and held different jobs. If you've had more than three jobs, be selective. List the three that do the most to make you an attractive applicant; then decide if any of the jobs that remain does more to promote your candidacy. List it if it does and omit it if it doesn't, unless your educational record is ordinary and you've participated in few, if any, extracurricular activities. Under these circumstances, your work experience is your only strong suit, so make it count. List every job you've had. It'll show that you're not afraid of work, and may suggest to some people that you're capable, resourceful, and determined.

Extracurricular Activities

If you've done some interesting things, this can be an important part of your resume, especially if you have little or no work experience. List your most impressive activities first. If you have the space, describe very briefly the key things you did. If you don't have the space to elaborate, don't worry about it. Trying to decide how to fit all the good things you've done onto one page is the kind of problem you want.

If you've participated in lots of activities, list only the four or five that are most likely to strengthen your image. If your extracurricular activities are thin, use a simple rule of thumb to decide which, if any, to include: will they enhance your resume and make you a stronger candidate for the jobs you want? If your work experience consists of summer jobs as waiter, camp counselor, and lifeguard, two or three extracurricular activities, however modest, can help. They'll indicate that you have interests which you pursue enthusiastically, and they may help to give you a well-rounded image. Remember, this section is optional. Include it only if you feel it will help.

Coursework

Coursework is a reliable area to fall back on if you have little or no work experience and few, if any, extracurricular activities. It'll give you something legitimate to say, fill the blank spaces on your resume, and possibly help you score points if the courses you list are clearly related to the work you're seeking.

If you want to include coursework on your resume, limit yourself to key courses in your major field of study, courses that are related to the jobs you're applying for, and special projects or internships that were related to the courses you took. For example, a graduating senior trying for an entry-level position in marketing research didn't have any relevant work experience, so she organized and presented her key courses in the following way:

COURSEWORK:

Psychology Methods of Psychological Research; Social Psychology; Theories of Motivation; Psychology and Communication; and Physiological Psychology.

Statistics Introductory Statistics; Regression and Correlation; Sampling; and Nonparametric Statistics.

Marketing Marketing Research Techniques; Consumer Behavior; **Research** and Advertising Research.

It's simple and straightforward, and it can work. Why? Because it tells potential employers that she understands the kinds of knowledge marketing research requires, that she tailored a program of study to these requirements, and that she completed the program. By itself, that can strengthen her candidacy and improve her chances of being interviewed. Coursework, like extracurricular activities, is optional. Use it if you think it'll help.

Skills

If you have any skills that aren't made clear by the things you say about your education, coursework, and work experience, spell them out in this section. You never know when a skill you don't think matters will tip the scale in your favor. Are you fluent in a second language? In a third? Do you write unusually well? Are you good with a camera? Are you an able public speaker? Can you handle a word processor? Do you have a flair for organizing events? Are you a fine swimmer? Put it down. It doesn't take up much space, and it may strike a chord with a potential employer.

Interests

This is another subject that can help you fill up the page. At the same time, it can help give the impression that you're well rounded. When should you include your interests on your resume? If you have strong academic credentials, took part in some interesting extracurricular activities, and held a few good jobs, it's unlikely that you'll have room to list your interests. And you don't really need to, because you've already made a persuasive case for your candidacy. On the other hand, if your educational record is ordinary, your extracurricular activities skimpy, and the jobs you've held pedestrian, put together—without fabricating—as impressive a list of interests as you can. Do you play the guitar? Do you run? Are you an avid reader? Do you travel? Do you ski? Ride horses? Play tennis? Play chess? Go to the theater a lot? Say so. It'll further define you and give potential employers a better sense of you as a person. And it may, when added to the other things you've done, impress someone enough to want to see you.

A word of caution: think carefully about listing interests that may mark you as eccentric, like collecting beetles, picking wild mushrooms, and breeding turtles. While each of these is a legitimate interest, each is also a bit off the beaten track. Unfortunately, a lot of companies have fairly conservative selection criteria, and one "unusual" interest can override the favorable image that everything else about you has helped to create. However, if you're applying for an offbeat job, one in which the organization is loosely structured and informal or people value the unusual and prize creativity, feel free to mention unique interests.

Professional Organizations

If you're a student member of a professional organization like the American Marketing Association, say so. It can only help.

References

There are a number of things you can say under the references section, all of them brief: "references available upon request" and "references furnished upon request" are a couple. Do not list the names, addresses, and phone numbers of your references. It's unprofessional, takes up valuable space on your resume, and allows potential employers to call your references before you've had a chance to tell them about the job and the company.

Don't choose your references haphazardly. Poorly chosen references can undo all the time and effort you've spent persuading an interviewer that you're an outstanding candidate for the job. When a decision is made to hire you pending a reference check, you don't want one of your references to say something that'll make the company have second thoughts. You do want every one of your references to say things that confirm what the interviewer knows and believes about you. So pick your references carefully. Try for one or two teachers and one or two people you've worked for who think highly of you and your work. Also see if you can get one or two people who know you personally, like you, and will say good things about you.

Tell these people that you'd like them to be your references, but only if they feel comfortable in that role. If they don't, you want them to tell you, not the representative of a company you want to work for. If you're not sure of someone after you've spoken to him, don't use that person as a reference. Use only those people you know you can count on.

THE DESIGN OF YOUR RESUME

The things you've done and how you describe them are the building blocks of your resume. The trick is to put them together in a way that's visually appealing, that makes people want to read your resume because of the way it looks. If you've got a terrific background, a poor layout isn't likely to hurt much. It *will* hurt if your background is less than brilliant. Quite simply, a resume that's well designed is more likely to be read and to get you interviews than a resume that's not.

How do you make your resume work visually? How do you design it so that it's balanced and uncluttered? So that it makes everything easy to see and read, highlights your achievements, and impresses the reader before he's even read a word? The sample resumes at the end of this chapter will show you how.

SOME ADDITIONAL GUIDELINES

1. Once your resume is typed, proofread it slowly, carefully, and repeatedly. Check for errors in spelling, punctuation, and spacing, and for missing words and sentences. Use your rough draft as a guide. It may seem like a waste of time to proofread a one-page resume four times. Do it. A fourth pass can turn up a typo, a missing comma, an extra space between words that you overlooked the first three times around.

2. Consider having your resume typeset, and at the very least have it reproduced on a machine that turns out high-quality copies. Tell the operator that you'd like to see a copy before he runs the entire job. Look it over carefully. Every letter, every number, every punctuation mark should be sharply defined and dark enough to be read at a glance, but not overly dark. Check for spots and other unwanted marks. Sometimes the glass screen through which your resume is photographed needs to be cleaned. If there's anything you're not happy with, say so, and don't permit your job to be run till it's fixed to your satisfaction.

3. Don't write *anything* by hand on your resume—not a comma, not a period, nothing.

4. Don't list your height, weight, health, marital status, age,

race, or religion on your resume. With the exception of your health, they have nothing to do with your ability to handle a job. And your health, barring a truly debilitating or incapacitating illness, is no one's business but your own.

5. Don't list the salary you'd like or expect to get. All it'll cause is trouble. If your number is higher than their number, you won't be interviewed. If it's lower, potential employers may feel that you have a poor sense of the marketplace or that you're desperate. Besides, any company that wants to hire you will discuss salary. So bide your time.

SAMPLE RESUMES

The resumes that follow will give you a sense of some of the many ways in which resumes can be written and designed.

SUSAN J. DUFFY

School address:
79 Hillcrest Hall
University of Pennsylvania
Philadelphia, PA 19106
(215) 627-1896

Permanent address:
177 Cartbridge Road
Atlanta, GA 30342
(404) 257-0378

EDUCATION

University of Pennsylvania, Philadelphia, PA
Annenberg School of Communications
B.A. in Visual Communications, 1989
GPA: 3.3 overall, 3.8 in major

ACTIVITIES

Association of Visual Communications
 • Faculty Relations Committee. Worked with faculty members to
   design programs for association members.
American Advertising Federation
 • Campbell Ewald Collegiate Competition. Created and submit-
   ted an advertising campaign for a fictitious soft drink.
Delta Phi Sorority
 • Chairperson, Philanthropy Committee
 • Arts and Entertainment Committee
Hope Church, Philadelphia, PA
 • Sunday School Teacher

EXPERIENCE

Technical Production Intern, Cablevision News 16, Atlanta, GA,
Summer, 1987, 1988. Responsibilities included getting the news set
ready, correcting and collating news scripts, and operating the
teleprompter during the live airing of each show.

INTERESTS

Theater, American art, sailing, golf

REFERENCES

Submitted upon request.

STEVEN MARCH

38 Darby Road
Rye, New York 10580
(914) 967-1858

EDUCATION

1989	**B.B.A.,** Iona College, New Rochelle, NY Major: Marketing GPA: 3.8
1987	**A.A.,** Westchester Community College, Valhalla, NY Major: Marketing GPA: 3.7 Financed 50% of college costs by working.

HONORS

1989	Maxwell Award, highest grade point in marketing
1989	McClain Award for the outstanding senior thesis in marketing
1988	Iona College Trustees Scholarship

EXPERIENCE

Spring, 1989 — **Intern,** New York State Department of Labor. Developed job descriptions, prepared a report that examined the rights of employees of the state government to strike, and helped coordinate a program designed to teach job interviewing skills to marginally educated applicants.

January 1987–February 1989 — **President,** Student House Painters, Rye, NY. Founded and built a nine-person house-painting company. Developed a market for the company's services, recruited student workers, negotiated contracts, scheduled jobs, and supervised work crews.

EXTRACURRICULAR ACTIVITIES

Marketing Club, vice-president. Coordinated membership drive and organized special projects.

REFERENCES

Submitted upon request.

PAUL DWYER

1709 LINDHURST DRIVE
DAYTON, OHIO 45449
(513) 433-8186

EDUCATION

1989	Texas Tech University, Lubbock, TX B.S. in Mechanical Engineering GPA in major: 4.0 Graduated magna cum laude
1985	Williams High School, Dayton, OH Honors graduate, top 1% of class, senior class president

EXPERIENCE

September, 1988– May, 1989	**Programmer,** Computer Center, Texas Tech Designed and implemented programs for the university's Alumni Center.
September, 1986– May, 1987	**Tutor,** Higher Education Opportunity Program, Texas Tech, Lubbock, TX. Tutored students in calculus, linear mathematics, and statistics.
Summer, 1986	**Customer Liaison,** Lakehurst Savings Bank, Dayton, Ohio. Managed early-bird window service, kept track of the daily inflow and outflow of cash, and helped customers resolve their banking problems.

HONORS

American Legion Award for outstanding academic achievement
National Honor Society
David Winslow Tuition Scholarship, 1987, 1988

INTERESTS

Tennis, racquetball, volleyball, calligraphy, trumpet

REFERENCES

References furnished upon request

DONALD SLOAN

Gates Hall
University of Kansas
Lawrence, KS 66045
(913) 243-1682

After May 1989:
46 Clayton Drive
St. Louis, MO 63130
(314) 726-8840

Education

B.A., University of Kansas, Lawrence, KS, 1989
Major: Social Services
Minor: Psychology

Experience

Assistant to Activities Supervisor, Fairview Nursing Home, Lawrence, KS, November 1987—May 1989. Helped organize and implement recreational activities for 75 nursing home residents: for example, crafts, sing-alongs, dances, day trips, and entertainment.
Hotline Volunteer, Teen Crisis Center, Lawrence, KS, September 1986—May 1987. Handled crisis calls from teenagers in the community.
Nurse's Aide, Danvers General Hospital, St. Louis, MO, Summer, 1985. Assisted nurses in patient care.

Activities

Student Affairs Committee
University Concert Board
Psychology Society
Residence Programming Board
Senior Gift Campaign

Skills

Fluent in French. Water safety instructor. Skilled at working with people.

Interests

Skiing, softball, classical music, and guitar.

References

Available upon request.

KENNETH WILSON
17 Beechmont Street
San Rafael, CA 94901   (415) 488-7403

Education	**University of Idaho,** Moscow, Idaho B.A. in English Literature, 1989
Activities	**Editor-in-chief,** Nexus, University of Idaho Yearbook. Directed a staff of 20 people. Supervised copy and artwork, layout, and publication. **Literary Club.** Read and discussed major twentieth-century novels. **Intercollegiate Volleyball Team,** 1987–1989. **Herald Society.** Hosted prospective students and led tours of the campus.
Experience	**Teacher's Assistant,** COPE Program, Moscow, Idaho, September 1988—May 1989. Worked with underprivileged junior high school students. Explained and corrected assignments, helped plan the agenda for each class, and worked with individual students to improve their math and reading skills. **Night Manager,** John's Food Store, Moscow, Idaho, September 1987—May 1988. Responsible for weekly inventory and control of stock, purchasing selected food and nonfood items, and tallying daily receipts.
Interests	Volleyball, tennis, photography, racquetball.
References	Available upon request.

CHAPTER THREE

How to Find Out Where the Jobs Are and Get Interviews

Your resume looks great. It's well written, well designed and makes a persuasive case for your candidacy. It's ready to go, be put in the hands of potential employers, and get you interviews. Which means you're ready to find out where the jobs are.

There are all sorts of ways to find out about jobs. The best ones seem to be:

- Networking
- The college placement office
- Classified ads
- Contacting companies
- Employment agencies
- The U.S. government

Let's look at each in detail.

NETWORKING

Never underestimate contacts. They can open doors that you'd never get near by yourself. Who qualifies as a contact? Anyone you know who might be able to help. That includes relatives, friends, neighbors, teachers, people you've worked for, and people your family knows.

Start by taking inventory. Make a list of all the people you know. Find out what kinds of work they do and who they work for. Focus on the ones who work in a field and/or for a company that interests you. If they're teachers, focus on the ones whose field you wish to enter.

Call them, bring them up to date on your status, ask to meet with them, but remember, you're only asking for advice at this point, not a job. If the person works or teaches in a field that interests you, say something like:

"I'm very interested in a career in marketing. I'd like to find out as much as I can about the field, and I felt you'd be a good person to talk to. Could we get together sometime to discuss it?"

If the person works for a company you'd like to work for, say something like:

"I've heard some good things about Allegheny Foods, and I'm thinking about applying for a job there. Before I do, I thought it would help if I talked to someone who knows a lot more about the company than I do. Could I meet with you sometime soon?"

People are flattered when someone expresses interest in the work they do. Most will be happy to meet with you, tell you things that will help, and be receptive when you tell them you'd like to drop off a copy of your resume in case they come across someone who's looking to fill an entry-level position. When you drop off your resume, leave several copies. Your contacts may need them.

Contacts can be an excellent source of interviews, because when they recommend you, it's to people they know. As a courtesy, if for no other reason, these people are more likely to see you. When they do, they'll probably tell you things you didn't know, things that will help; they may lead you to other people and other job opportunities; and they may, if the interview goes unusually well, make you an offer.

Perhaps the most important thing about networking is to let people know that you're "looking"—when you're at a party, waiting on line in the supermarket, working out in a local gym, or having a cavity filled by your dentist. You never know who people know. Your dentist may have a brother-in-law or a patient who's an editor in a publishing company. Or your minister may be friendly with your congressman, which could give you a leg up if you're looking for a way into local government.

To get these people to help you, it's imperative that you make a good impression on them. Since they may not be in the field you want to get into, they're going to have to like you personally, not professionally. Aside from being friendly and interested, you might also try to develop a pattern of helping people, of making yourself useful, whether it's giving someone a lift, asking if they need something from the hardware store while you're there, or offering to help shovel a driveway after a heavy snowstorm. No, it's not Machiavellian, it's just smart. You can't get far in this world without help from others, help you won't get if they think you don't deserve it.

Afterward, don't forget to send a thank-you note to those who helped you. Not only is it the right thing to do, but it'll make it easier to approach the person again if you need to.

THE COLLEGE PLACEMENT OFFICE

Most college placement offices offer graduating seniors an unparalleled opportunity: to interview with major corporations on campus. Each spring, thousands of companies recruit at colleges and universities across the country. The college placement office prepares a schedule of companies, the positions they're trying to fill, the dates they'll be on campus, and the deadline for submitting resumes. The companies review the resumes they receive and make appointments with the students they wish to see. If a recruiter feels that a student he's interviewed is worth pursuing, the student is invited, at the company's expense, to spend a day meeting people at the company.

Imagine! Companies come to your school, tell you what they're looking for, encourage you to submit a resume, and, if they're interested, invite you to interview. It's a wonderful opportunity, and it comes only once. After you graduate, you compete with hundreds, sometimes thousands of people for a hearing. You send letters, make phone calls, visit employment agencies to get what the placement office is handing you on a platter: the opportunity to secure more interviews with potential employers than you'll be able to scare up in three months of hustling after you graduate. So read the schedule of campus interviews carefully, try for as many interviews as you can, and prepare for each interview as if it's the only one you have.

Many schools also post or record career opportunities in or near the placement office. If your school is among them, check their listings on a regular basis before you graduate. If you can, check it after you graduate, too.

CLASSIFIED ADS

Classified ads are the most accessible source of information about job openings. All you have to do is buy the Sunday edition of a major metropolitan newspaper, like *The New York Times*. An entire section of the paper is devoted to classified ads for all kinds of jobs. Look under "college grads." It's where most entry-level positions are located.

Besides newspapers, two other kinds of publications carry classified ads. Though they seldom list positions that don't require any experience, these publications can be very useful if you've done some work in the field. They are:

   • Trade papers. For example, job openings in the field of advertising are carried by *Advertising Age* and *Adweek,* both weekly publications. In the field of fashion, look at *Women's Wear Daily*. The information desk at any good-sized library should be able to direct you to the leading trade publications in most fields. If they can't, try the *Standard Rate and Data Business Publication Directory*.

- The news periodicals of professional associations. For example, *Marketing News*, which is published biweekly by the American Marketing Association, carries ads for all kinds of positions in marketing and marketing research. The *Encyclopedia of Associations* lists the names, addresses, and phone numbers of more than 1,200 associations. Find the ones in your field and call. Ask if they publish a news periodical, if it contains job listings, and where you can find it.

When you start to look at classified ads, you'll find three kinds:

- Company ads, which are placed by the companies themselves. These ads include the company name and address, usually describe the job in some detail, and instruct applicants to submit resumes to the company.
- Blind company ads, which differ from company ads in one way: they don't include the company's name and address. Instead, applicants are directed to send resumes to a box number at the publication in which the ad appears.
- Employment agency ads. Employment agencies earn commissions when people who they recruit, screen, and submit to client firms are hired. The ads they place are a first step in the process, and are designed to bring in potential applicants.

Follow one rule of thumb: throw a wide net and throw it quickly. Don't make the mistake of holding out for a job listing that you're perfect for. Don't wait till you see an ad for a job that meets all your requirements. No ad tells you everything, and many ads can be misleading. So apply. You have nothing to lose but time. If an ad looks at all interesting, submit a resume immediately. Lots of other people will. If you wait, the job may be gone before your resume gets there.

CONTACTING COMPANIES

There are several things to be said for submitting an unsolicited resume to potential employers:

- You can pick the companies you'd like to work for.
- You get to test the waters before you graduate, if you wish to.
- The cover letter you write will give you a chance to say things your resume doesn't, to make a more persuasive case for your candidacy.

Writing to companies has just two drawbacks. The first is that you normally don't know if the companies you've chosen have job openings that you qualify for. Don't worry about it, and don't let it stop you. Remember, all you want is one job. And someone is often quitting, getting transferred, getting fired, or retiring. If you submit resumes to sixty companies, get six interviews, and receive one offer, you've succeeded.

The second drawback is that lots of other people will be doing the same thing. There are about 1.2 million college graduates each year, many of whom write to companies for jobs. The result of all this letter writing is that companies are often flooded with resumes. Unless yours is exceptional, you obviously have a better chance of being interviewed by a company that gets 50 resumes than by one that gets 5,000. Which companies tend to be targeted by relatively few people? Small companies, companies that not many people are aware of. So take a flyer if you want to and send some resumes to the corporate giants, but make sure you write to small companies, too, ones you might never have heard of but that are perhaps more likely than the big ones to consider you for a job.

How do you put together a list of companies? You start by answering two questions:

- What kinds of industries or fields interest you? For example, communications? Politics? Transportation? Packaged goods? Music?
- Where do you want to work? The Midwest? The Northeast? The South? In a major city? In a smaller city? In a suburb?

Once you've answered these questions, head for the library and ask to see the most recent edition of *The National Job Bank: A Comprehensive Guide to Major Employers in the Nation's Key Job Markets*. The *Job Bank* carries job opportunities in 10,000 companies, which are organized by the ten major regional job markets in the country. Within each region, the *Job Bank* lists company names, addresses, phone numbers, the products and/or services that the company markets, the areas in which the company is hiring, and the person to contact. There's also a cross-index that breaks employers down into thirty-one industrial categories such as engineering services, computer-related positions, banking, broadcasting, and health care.

A second source of company names and possible jobs is the *Career Employment Opportunities Directory*. The directory consists of four volumes, each containing job opportunities for graduates in the following subject areas: liberal arts and social sciences, business administration, the sciences, and engineering and computer sciences. Listed is the name of each company, a brief description of the company, a detailed description of the career opportunities that the company offers, and the person to contact for additional information.

If you want to broaden your focus a bit, take a look at the *Standard Directory of Advertisers*. There are two volumes, one organized geographically; the other by industry. Both contain information on thousands of companies that advertise. If you want to broaden your focus a lot, try the *Million Dollar Directory: America's Leading Public and Private Companies*. It consists of three volumes and contains information about 115,000 businesses, each worth at least a half-million dollars. It'll tell you what each company sells, its annual sales, how many people it employs, the names of its top people, and its address and phone number. If there's a specific industry that you'd like to become part of, such as advertising, banking, or stock brokerage, find out which association represents the industry you've chosen. They'll be able to tell you the name of the industry directory and where you can find it.

If you want to go after a job in a field that may not be covered by these directories, such as education, social service, communications, the arts, or health care, there are other directories that can help. For example:

- *The Working Press of the Nation* is a four-volume directory that contains information on more than 8,400 radio and television stations, on more than 4,800 magazines, and on newspapers, news services, and photo services throughout the country.
- *Literary Market Place* provides listings of most book publishers and literary agencies in the country.
- *The National Directory for the Performing Arts and Civic Centers* lists organizations whose business is the performing arts.
- The federal government issues three directories— *Education Directory: Colleges and Universities, Education Directory: Public School Systems*, and *Education Directory: State Education Agency Officials*—that list every accredited two- and four-year college, public elementary and secondary schools throughout the country, and key officers of education agencies.
- The *National Directory of Private Social Agencies* contains listings on more than 14,000 agencies. Listings include the areas in which they provide services and a description of the services they offer.
- The *American Hospital Association Guide to the Health Care Field* contains information on thousands of hospitals and health-related organizations.

Get the names, addresses, and phone numbers of about sixty companies that meet your criteria and call each one. Ask for the name of the person who heads the department you'd like to join: for example, Director of Marketing, Director of Research and Development, or Director of Management Information Systems. If you're not sure how to spell the person's name, ask. If you're not sure what department you want, ask to speak to someone in the Personnel Department. They'll tell you. Even if the name of the person you want is listed in the directory you use, call. These listings are about a year old, and people change jobs. When you call, say that you'd like some information, then ask for the name you want. Most companies will be happy to help.

You're ready to write to each company. All that's missing is a cover letter. A cover letter has two objectives: to tell the person to whom you're writing why you're writing and to persuade him to see you. Can a cover letter make a difference? It sure can. Your resume, however well prepared, is essentially a fact sheet that follows established form. In a cover letter, you can say anything you wish. You can be simple and straightforward, you can be witty, you can be forceful, you can even be compelling. You can tie a childhood interest in the company's products to your wish to work for them now, you can play off your admiration for the company's commitment to technological development, or you can talk about your background and how it'll help you contribute to the company's growth. A cover letter gives you an opportunity to say things that'll mark you as special, that'll make people want to look at your resume, that'll make them want to meet you.

There are two kinds of cover letters you can write. One says you're applying for a job. The other is less direct. Rather than asking to work for the company, you ask to meet with the person you're writing to because you want to find out more about his industry and his profession. Why take this approach? If you apply for a job and the company has no openings, they might not see you. However, they may see you if you say that your purpose is to gather information. If they do, you'll find out things about the industry you didn't know, you may pick up some leads, and, if you're sufficiently impressive, they may even create a position for you because they think you're too good to let go.

Does this mean that all your cover letters should request meetings to learn more about the industry? Not at all. If a company has openings, applying for a job is the best thing you can do. Letters requesting meetings to acquire information are designed to get you some interviews even if the letters you send that apply for jobs don't. So mix it up. Send letters that apply for jobs to forty-five companies and letters that ask for meetings to discuss the industry to fifteen.

Each letter you send should cover the following ground:

- Why you're writing. Because you want to apply for a position or learn about the person's industry and profession.
- Why you're writing to this particular company. Possible reasons are the quality of their products, the business they're in, the fact that they're growing, their innovativeness, and their reputation for giving employees every opportunity to grow.
- Why they should see you. Use whatever you think will help most to make your case: for example, facets of your background, key personality traits and/or what you want in a job.
- That you'd like to arrange a meeting.

Close each letter in the same way. Tell the person to whom you're writing that you've enclosed your resume for his review and that you'll call shortly to determine his interest in meeting you. That way, you're in a position to get an answer to each letter you send.

Before you send your cover letter and resume to anyone, have someone whose judgment you respect critique the letter, especially if someone else has written or polished your resume. You want to make sure that the quality of both your resume and your cover letter is consistently high.

Call each of the people to whom you sent letters about a week after you mailed them. If the person you're calling is away from his desk or out of the office, leave your name and say you'll call again. If he's on another line, tell his secretary you'll wait, and do, for ten minutes if necessary. The chances are good he'll take your call. Don't let a secretary take your number and tell you he'll return your call. He won't. Keep calling back till you get through. Most of the people you're trying to reach don't spend a lot of free time at their desks. They're on the phone, at meetings, out of town. So expect to make a number of calls before you get through. Try to call right around 8:45 A.M. or just after lunch, at about 2:00 or 2:30. These are the times of day when people in positions of responsibility are most likely to be available.

EMPLOYMENT AGENCIES

There are two kinds of employment agencies: privately run agencies and agencies operated by state and federal governments. Both types try to place job applicants in positions listed by employers.

Private Employment Agencies

Wherever there are jobs, there are private employment agencies. If you use them, keep several things in mind:

- Agencies tend to specialize, handling positions in specific fields: for example, finance, publishing, commercial art, and health care; and in placing recent college graduates. To find out which agencies handle recent college graduates and which ones place people in the field you want to get into, pick up the leading paper in the area where you want to work and look at the listings in the classified section. Other sources of employment agencies are the Yellow Pages and a directory that you can get by writing to the National Employment Association of Personnel Consultants, 1012 14th Street N.W., Washington, DC 20006.
- Many of the entry-level jobs that agencies carry will fall short of your expectations—unless you expect to type.

The typical entry-level job description begins with glowing phrases about opportunity and involvement, then ends with "type 60 wpm." Don't get discouraged. Some of these jobs are worth taking, because if you're good, they'll lead to bigger and better things. Others are dead-end spots. Learn to tell the difference between the two. Find out how much time you'll be expected to spend typing, how much time you'll have to do other things, and what those other things will be. Ask how soon you'll be able to move from the typewriter to a full-time position on the professional staff. If the answers you get are evasive, stay away.

- Some of the entry-level jobs that agencies list are good ones, ones worth pursuing. So let them know who you are. Send a resume and cover letter asking for an interview, then follow up with a call.

- When agencies make placements, they get paid—by the employer, by the applicant, or by both. The fees for filling the vast majority of jobs that college graduates apply for are paid by employers. Still, don't take any chances. Ask. If they tell you you're responsible for the fee, look elsewhere.

- Don't let an agency push you into a job you don't want. Agencies get paid for putting people into jobs. If they don't have a job you want, some agencies will try to persuade you to apply for one you don't want. And they'll say all kinds of things to get you there, seductive things, intimidating things, things like, "You're a bright kid. Once they see what you can do, they'll move you into a great spot." Or, "The job market is pretty bad, and you have to start somewhere. This is as good a place as any." Or, "You've got to get some experience. Once you do, you'll be able to get what you want." Don't buy any of it. A job you don't want can mean doing things you don't like, in which you're not interested, or at which you're not good. It can mean working for someone you neither like nor respect. It can mean a long, unpleasant commute.

So keep looking and remember, taking a job you don't want is a last resort.

State and Federal Employment Agencies

State and federal employment agencies list all kinds of jobs with private and publicly held companies. Some of these jobs may be right for you. To find out if there's an office nearby, check your local telephone directory.

THE U.S. GOVERNMENT

The federal government is far and away the single largest employer in the country, so it always has jobs to fill. The source of information about these jobs is a Federal Job Information Center. To find out where the nearest one is, call 1-800-555-1212.

CHAPTER FOUR

How to Get Ready for
an Interview

One day it happens. One of the resumes you sent, one of the letters you wrote, one of the calls you made gets you an interview. You make an appointment, then hang up amid feelings of elation and anxiety. It's what you wanted. Without it, no one's going to hire you. You feel like celebrating, until you realize it's not something you're really looking forward to. You're thinking: "What will they ask me? What should I say? What should I ask them?" You've asked yourself some good questions. Let's look at how you're going to answer them.

DEFINE YOUR OBJECTIVES

Let's start with your objectives, what you want to achieve when you interview. You should approach the job interview with two broad objectives.

Your first objective is to present yourself as favorably as you can without being dishonest; that is, without saying things about yourself that aren't true. That doesn't mean you shouldn't be selective in what you tell the interviewer. On the contrary. Always be selective. Always tell the interviewer the best things you can about yourself. Never volunteer information about the worst. The company that's interviewing you certainly won't. They want to hire the best person they can. To do that, the interviewer will present the company in as favorable a light as he can. Your game plan should be no different.

Your second objective is to find a job, a company, and a community that provides the right fit. You want the job you take to be a rewarding experience, personally as well as professionally. You want to like the work you do, the opportunities for growth, the people you work with and for, the salary you earn, and the city or town where you live and work. What you like and don't like will depend primarily on who and what you are: your abilities, your aspirations, your personality, and your values. It's up to you to have a good sense of who you are, what you want and don't want, what you can live with and what you can't. For example, don't take a job in Festus, Missouri, if nightlife is a priority. And if you enjoy the quiet of the country, if noise, crowds, and traffic make you grit your teeth, stay away from Manhattan.

Armed with a pretty good sense of yourself and your priorities, find out as much as you can about the job, the company and, if necessary, the community; then decide if the fit is a good one. If you feel it is, your job is to persuade the interviewer that you're what this company wants and needs, that the fit between you and the job is outstanding.

The best way to achieve these objectives is to prepare, as you would for an exam, an athletic contest, or an artistic performance—with thought, care, and effort.

HOW TO PREPARE FOR THE THINGS INTERVIEWERS LOOK FOR AND THE QUESTIONS THEY ASK

If they're good, interviewers will try to find out several things about you:

1. How you present yourself, or the impression you make.
2. How bright or intelligent you are.
3. What you've done—your educational experiences, work experiences, participation in the community, and special accomplishments.
4. How committed you are to work. Are you willing to work hard to do what it takes to excel in this job?
5. The kind of person you are. Are you mature? Stable? Responsible? Do you have a healthy sense of your own worth? Are you enthusiastic? Energetic? Confident? Trustworthy?

Interviewers will try to shed light on these aspects of you by observing you and by asking questions. The ground they'll cover includes the following:

What You Look Like

Care about how you look, because it can matter a lot. How should you dress? The first thing to realize is that there's no formula, no one best way to dress. It really depends on the kind of job you're applying for. One way to find out is to ask. If you know someone who works in the field you're trying to get into, ask him what people who do this type of work normally wear and what dress would be appropriate for an interview.

If you're a man, and if the job you're applying for is the first step on a managerial or executive track, wear a dark blue two- or three-piece suit that's recently been dry cleaned, a clean and ironed white dress shirt, a dark blue tie either striped or quietly patterned, black socks, and polished black dress shoes. If you choose to wear after-shave or cologne, wear a scent that's conservative, subdued, and won't overpower the interviewer. However, if you're trying for a job that's on a somewhat different track, say an assistant to a creative director in a small, innovative advertising agency, you have considerably more leeway, and you should use it. Wear clothes that set you apart from the pack, that make a statement about your creative instincts. It can be a bowtie, a turtleneck with stylishly contrasting jacket and pants, or an interesting haircut, as long as it says that you're plugged into today's trends.

If you're a woman, the same rule of thumb applies: tailor your dress to the requirements of the job. And remember, creative—but not outlandish—attire can impress others with your sense of style as well as your self-confidence. So don't be afraid to be a bit different, even if you're applying for a mainstream white-collar position. Wear a bright color or a natty houndstooth instead of the regulation pinstripe. If you can carry it off, they'll remember you.

Whether you're a man or a woman, bring an attaché case. While it doesn't have to be leather and gold tooled, it shouldn't be pasteboard and clearly worn. An attaché case will help you convey a sense of professionalism. It will also transport the things you'll want to bring with you: several copies of your resume, an 8½×11-inch ruled pad, a pen, a typed list of your references, a hairbrush and/or comb, a pack of breath mints, and any other last-minute aids you might need. For example, if you sometimes get pre-interview jitters and your lips get parched, a stick of lip balm is a good thing to have along.

Your Body Language

Body language can create all kinds of impressions. To make your body language work for you:

- Smile when you meet the interviewer, look into his eyes, shake hands firmly but not so firmly that you make him wince, and say something like: "Hello. My name is Michelle Jones. Glad to meet you."
- When you stand or walk, stand straight. Don't slouch.

- When you're sitting, your posture should be open, not defensive. For example, don't wrap your arms around your body as if you were hugging yourself, and don't hunch forward as if you're about to leap from your seat.
- Don't fidget. Don't swing a foot, tap your fingers, play with jewelry, or fiddle with your nails.
- Maintain eye contact with the interviewer no matter who's doing the talking.
- Look like you're paying attention. Don't look like your mind is wandering.

Each of these behaviors has nothing to do with what you say or how you say it, yet each conveys information about you to the interviewer: information about how poised, confident, assertive, and attentive you are.

How You Speak

Essentially, two things count:

- Sound like you care. Whatever you say, whatever words you use, if you don't sound like you care you'll hurt your chances of getting the job. This doesn't mean that everything you say must bubble over—too much can be as bad as none at all. But it does mean that you want to speak forcefully and with conviction at key moments; for example, when you're talking about an important event or turning point in your life; when you're talking about what you want in a job or why you want this particular job; and when you're trying to convince the interviewer that you have the ability and the determination to do the job better than anyone else. In short, you have to be "up" for each interview, you have to treat it like it's the best chance you'll ever have to get a job. If you don't, you're wasting an opportunity as well as your time.
- Speak clearly, confidently, and at a reasonable pace. Don't mumble or talk in a voice that's so low you can barely be heard. Don't talk too quickly or too slowly.

Don't say "um," "like," or "you know" a lot. Don't speak hesitantly, as if you're unsure of the value of what you're saying. Because if the interviewer has to strain to hear you, fight to keep up with you because you're racing along, or feels that getting words out of you is like pulling teeth, he'll be less than impressed.

What You Say

Every interviewer is going to expect you to give answers whose meanings are clear and to the point. This checklist will help you decide if you have any weaknesses:

- Can you organize your thoughts and express them clearly, or do you have difficulty putting together a coherent sentence?
- Can you use grammatically correct English when you're interviewed?
- Do you talk too much? Do you say too little, offering "yes," "no," and other brief replies?
- Do you answer questions clearly or are you vague, uncertain, and disorganized?
- Are your answers to the point or are they evasive?
- Are you familiar with the jargon of the field you want to enter? If you're not, head for the library and read a few of the recent issues of the leading trade magazine or paper. Then try to find someone who works in this field. When you do, ask him to tell you about the business his company's in, the nature of that business, and the kinds of things his company does. If he's like most people, his conversation will be peppered with the jargon of his field.

Your Education

The interviewer will probably ask you a fair number of questions about your college years. His questions are likely to include the following:

Why did you go to the college or university you did?
You probably have good reasons of your own. If you'd like to add
to them, here are some possibilities. Talk about the quality of
the department in which you majored. If you went to a large
school, talk about wanting to meet different kinds of people and
wanting access to the many cultural events that a large university
offers. If you went to a small school, talk about wanting to go to
a school whose faculty was more concerned with teaching than
research, at which classes were small, and at which no one got
lost in the crowd. Don't give reasons that run counter to the
image you want to convey: for example, your best friend went
there so you did too, the school was close to home, or the
academic program didn't seem too difficult to handle.

Did you transfer from one school to another? If so, why?
Stick to positive reasons for transferring. For example: you
wanted a stronger department in your major field; you wanted to
be part of a more diverse student body; or you wanted to be
close to/in a major metropolitan area. Do not say things like, "I
didn't like the people I met," "The academic standards were too
high," or "I wanted to be close to home" (unless you were
needed at home to care for someone or help support your
family).

**Which courses did you like best? Which did you like least?
Why?**
When you talk about courses you liked, try to talk about ones
that relate to the company's business and ones that deal with
relevant skills: for example, a course in economics, a course that
taught you to write, a public speaking course, courses that made
you think both logically and creatively, and courses that challenged you. Spend little or no time talking about courses you
disliked. Going into detail about courses you didn't care about
only conveys negatives. It may imply that you're weak in those
areas, that you don't try very hard when you don't like something, that you work only when understanding comes easily. If
you do talk about courses you disliked, give the interviewer
reasons that won't hurt you: for example, the instructor didn't

know the field very well, was a bad teacher, or was absent a great deal.

What were the high points of your college years?

These should include courses that fired your imagination, teachers that inspired you, and participation in groups, events, and/or sports that were particularly rewarding. Do not mention things like the food fight at the student union or the two-day beer blast in your junior year.

What was your grade point average?

If your grade point average is less than impressive, try to find acceptable reasons why. For example, it took you a year or two to find your way academically. Once you did, your grades soared. Or you focused attention on those subjects that you really cared about, then spent the rest of your time on activities that would broaden your experiences as a person, such as the college newspaper, a sport, a musical instrument, photography, books, and so on.

Did you do as well academically as you could have?

Since most people don't realize their potential, the answer to this question will normally be "no." But a "no" doesn't mean you can't turn this question to your advantage. For example, you might say that your primary objective during your college years was growth as a well-rounded person—intellectually, culturally, athletically, and emotionally. Then expand a bit on this theme. If you worked to help pay for your education, say so, and make the point that though working kept you from spending as much time as you wanted to on coursework, it enabled you to earn your degree.

What did you do besides go to classes, write papers, and take exams?

Focus on things that you feel make you special, that are good indicators of traits or abilities that matter to you and will matter to the people you work for. Even if you haven't done much, find a couple of things that look good, then make them work for you.

Did it take you more than four years to graduate? If so, why?
Again, accentuate the positive. For example, "It took me a while
to find a major I really cared about. When I did, I wanted to take
all the courses I could. So I stayed in school an extra term." Or,
"I transferred because I was looking for a better art department
than the one I was in. When I found it, I stayed till I learned all
they could teach me."

Your Job History

If you have a job history, you're likely to be asked at least
some of the following questions:

Why did you take the jobs you did? Why did you leave?
If the jobs are full time, reasons like, "I took the job because I
felt I'd learn a lot" and "I felt the company would be an exciting
place to work" will take you a lot further than reasons like "the
money was good" and "it was the best I could do."

Take the same approach in your reasons for leaving: for
example, "There weren't any real opportunities for growth" and
"The job allowed me to give much less of myself than I wanted
to."

What did you spend most of your time doing?
Talk about concrete experiences that are most likely to be valued
by the company that's interviewing you, experiences that dem-
onstrate your ability to learn, to work well under pressure, to get
things done, to work well with others, to do more than you're
asked to do.

What did you like? What did you dislike?
You should like things that challenged you, that taught you, that
helped you to grow: for example, challenging assignments, work
that was different from what you had done, and working with
people who were bright, committed, and cared about their
work. Limit your dislikes to things that won't suggest that you're
hard to get along with, hard to please, not eager to extend

yourself, or more interested in short hours and comfortable working conditions than opportunities for growth.

How did you feel about the person you reported to?

Telling the interviewer that you didn't like or didn't get along with your former boss won't do you any good at all. What it will do is suggest that *you're* hard to get along with. So focus on the positive aspects of your relationship with your former boss, and create the impression that the relationship was a good one.

If you haven't had any jobs—and that includes summer jobs such as waiter, camp counselor, and lifeguard—be prepared to give the interviewer at least one good reason why.

What You Want in a Job

If you're pretty ambitious, bright, and confident, you should want a job that will:

- Interest you.
- Challenge you, teach you, and enable you to grow.
- Offer you increasing amounts of independence and the chance to make decisions.
- Provide you with opportunities to contribute to the company's effort to excel.
- Enable you to work with and for talented people who care about their work and are committed.
- Pay you fairly, and reward you for your contributions.

The first five items on this list will mark you as a person who has thought about what you want, is committed, is willing to work hard, and clearly has potential for growth. The last item on this list will tell the interviewer that you expect to be paid fairly for all this commitment, ability, and potential.

One more thing. When you say things like "I want a chance to grow," be prepared to elaborate, to tell the interviewer how you want to grow. If you can't, it'll just come off sounding like an empty platitude.

Why You Want to Leave Your Present Job

If you currently have a full-time job, the interviewer will want to know why you want to leave it. Your answer should focus on things like wanting to learn more than your present job can teach you; wanting more responsibility than your present job provides; wanting to work in a more challenging, stimulating environment; and wanting a job that provides more opportunities for career growth. Do not cite as reasons things like having a boss you can't stand, not getting along with your co-workers, disliking an office without windows, or wanting better health and life insurance coverage. Interviewers are impressed by people who want greater opportunities to contribute and grow, not by people who list among their concerns nicer places to work and better benefits.

Why You Want this Job

Stress two things:

- The outstanding fit between the requirements of the job and your ability to fulfill them.
- Your feeling that this company is an excellent place to work. Support this statement with several things about the company that impress you: for example, the company's reputation as a leader in its field, the company's rate of growth, the opportunities for professional growth that it provides, and its reputation as a place that cares about its staff.

Your Long-Term Aspirations

If you know what your career objectives are and how you hope to achieve them, you won't have any trouble answering this question. However, if you're unsure of where you want to get to and what the road is going to look like, don't feel that you have to lay out a well-articulated ten- or twenty-year plan. Rather, talk in generalities. For example:

- Talk about growing professionally by taking on a broad range of tasks.
- Talk about wanting to manage people and moving into increasingly responsible managerial positions.
- Talk about wanting opportunities that will enable you to make increasingly valuable contributions to the company.

The Questions You Ask

Do you ask enough questions? Are they clearly stated? Are they good ones? We'll look at just what these questions should be in a little while.

Your Answer to the Question, "Why Should We Hire You?"

This can be an intimidating question if you let it. Don't! Instead, make a brief, forceful case for your candidacy. Summarize the key requirements of the job, then make it clear that you have the ability, training, and personality to more than satisfy these requirements. For example, you might say, "Because I'm the right person for this job. You want someone who can work well as part of a team, who can analyze information and draw implications that make a difference, who can take the initiative when it needs to be taken, and who can earn the trust and confidence of your clients. I can do all these things and do them well. What I want is the chance to do them for [company name]." If you can, add briefly to this statement by citing some of the things you've done that suggest that you could indeed "do all these things and do them well."

How You Feel About People

To find this out, the interviewer may ask questions like these:

- Think about some of the people you really like, then tell me why you like them.

- Think about some people you don't like, then tell me why you feel that way.
- What qualities do you admire in others?

Try to focus on traits that companies value. For example, "The people I like are thinkers and doers. They're interesting to talk to and be with. They're also people I can count on, trust, and learn from." Stay away from statements like "I like her because she's wild, a lot of fun, and tells great stories."

The Kind of Person You Are

All the observations of you that the interviewer makes and all the answers you give to his questions help the interviewer to get a sense of the kind of person you are. To find out even more, the interviewer is likely to ask you a number of questions. Here are some examples:

Describe yourself.

Stress traits that are consistent with the image you've been creating. For example, "I'm inquisitive, I like to learn. I'm a hard worker. Whatever I do I want to do well. I like to think there's a solution to every problem, and I usually keep looking till I find it. I like people. I like sports, good books, and good music. I like to stretch, to see just how much I can do and how far I can go." Do not choose this time to bare your soul and say things like, "I sometimes get down on myself" or, "Deep inside, I question the value of this kind of work" or, "The day I win the lottery is the day I retire." Remember, the interviewer is listening for reasons to reject you as well as reasons to hire you.

What are some of the things that motivate you?

Include the desire to learn, grow as a person and as a professional, achieve, test your limits, and be the best that you can be.

How do you spend your free time?
Focus on things that foster personal growth and help make you well rounded: for example, books, sports, cinema, music, hobbies like photography, and involvement in your community.

What are your strengths?
If you're asked this question, don't feel compelled to list every strength you think you have. Rather, stick to the ones that are your best and that have the most to do with the job you're applying for.

What are your weaknesses?
Everyone has weaknesses. If you claim that you don't, you invite the conclusion that you're defensive. So own up, but do it in a way that's not likely to hurt you, and if you can, do it in a way that'll make you look good. Mention a couple of weaknesses that are likely to be viewed as assets. For example, you might say, "I set very high standards for myself, and sometimes they get in the way—like when I'm not given enough time to do a job well. Or when I work with someone who doesn't care about the quality of his work." As with flattery, the interviewer may not entirely believe you, but he wants to hear these things. Don't disappoint him. Never reveal unquestionable weaknesses like, "I get bored easily" or, "Sometimes I get lazy" or, "I don't like to be told what to do." And never give an interviewer a sob story. Interviewers want examples of determination and fortitude, not failure in the face of misfortune.

FINDING OUT ABOUT THE JOB, THE COMPANY, AND THE COMMUNITY

At some point, the interviewer will normally ask you if you have any questions. Unless he's made an unusually thorough presentation, your answer should be "yes."

There are two things you should find out as much as you can about: the job and the company. If the company is located in a place with which you're not familiar and you're going to have to move there if you take the job, you also will want to find out as much as you can about the community. Within reason, find out as much as you can about the job, the company, and, if need be, the community before you go on the interview. Find out the rest when you're there by listening to the interviewer and asking questions.

Questions about the job that you should try to get answers to are as follows:

1. How does the company describe the job? What kinds of things will they want you to do?
2. What skills and abilities does the job seem to require?
3. If the job is part of a group or department, how is the group or department structured, and what place in this structure does the job occupy?
4. What are the opportunities for growth?
5. What does the job pay? It's the interviewer's responsibility to bring up the issue of salary. There are two ways he can do that. He can tell you what the job pays, or he can ask you what your salary requirements are. If he does neither, you've got a decision to make: to ask or to remain silent. If your overriding goal is to get a job, don't ask. If the company wants to hire you, they'll raise the issue of salary at some point. It could be during your first interview, it could be during your third. However, if you feel you're in demand and you've decided on the lowest salary you'll accept, and if this company has a reputation for interviewing a candidate several times before discussing salary, take the bull by the horns and ask. Unfortunately, the interviewer will probably put the ball back in your court by asking you what you want. You can answer with a figure you think is fair, or you can answer by saying that you're not sure what a fair salary for this type of job is and that you'd like to know what the company is

offering. Given a choice, you're better off finding out, before the interview, what salary range the kind of position you're applying for normally pays. Armed with this information:

- You know what you can ask for and what you can expect to get.
- You won't sell yourself at less than market value and regret it later.
- You won't price yourself out of the market by asking for a salary that's beyond the range that the job pays.

To arrive at a fair number or to find out how much the kind of job you're applying for normally pays:

- Try to get information from your college placement service.
- Talk to friends who've applied for or gotten jobs that are like the one you're interested in.
- Talk to people you know who work in the field you want to enter.
- Look at the classified section in the Sunday edition of any major newspaper (e.g., *The New York Times*). It contains a great many job listings and salaries.

6. Are there other sources of income, such as bonuses, profit sharing, a savings plan, and a pension plan?
7. What about vacation? Two weeks with pay is customary.
8. Different forms of insurance are also customary, such as medical and disability. However, you may first have to pay a deductible.

Questions about the company that you should try to get answers to are as follows:

1. What's the company's reputation?
2. What products or services do they sell?
3. Who are their major competitors?
4. Is it a large, medium-sized, or small firm?
5. Are they growing? Are they profitable? What are their plans for the future?

6. How do they treat their employees? For example, what are the working conditions? Is there much turnover?
7. What kind of training, if any, do they offer?

One way to find out about a company is to call their public relations department and ask them to send you information. Most companies will be happy to do so. Another way is to visit your local library and get information from references like *Moody's Industrial Manual* and *Million Dollar Directory*. A third way is to read about the company in business publications, trade papers, and periodicals: for example, *Business Week, The Wall Street Journal, Advertising Age,* and *Publishers Weekly.* A fourth way is to talk to people who work in the industry and who know something about the company. A fifth way, and usually the best, is to talk to people who actually work for the company or who have worked there.

Questions about the community that you should try to get answers to are as follows:

1. How acceptable is the cost of living?
2. Can you find housing that you like?
3. Is the climate to your liking?
4. What about social, cultural, and recreational opportunities?
5. If you have children or plan to, how good are the schools?
6. How much time will you have to spend commuting? How comfortable and reliable are the available forms of transportation?
7. If you want to pursue an advanced degree, is there a university nearby?

There are several ways to get information about an area with which you're not familiar, short of visiting:

1. Read the *Places Rated Almanac* by Richard Boyer and David Savageau. It looks at the climates, housing, education, recreation, arts, crime rates, economic conditions, and transportation systems in about 300 metropolitan areas.

2. Write to the chamber of commerce.
3. Send for some copies of the local paper.
4. Write to local realtors for housing information.
5. Pay a visit to your library and do some research.

REHEARSING

One last thing you want to do when you're preparing thoroughly for job interviews is rehearse. Think about the questions you're likely to be asked, think about the answers you want to give, and think about the questions you want to ask. Then practice, and remember, a rehearsal shouldn't be an attempt to duplicate an actual interview. There's no way you can do that. Rather, rehearsals are designed to make you think through and work out the kinds of answers you'll want to give when you're interviewed. Rehearsing should also make you more comfortable with being asked questions about yourself and your feelings, and with answering them.

There are several ways to rehearse:

1. With someone else. Make a list of the questions that an interviewer might ask, then do mock interviews with a family member or friend acting as the interviewer.
2. By yourself. Read each question, then answer it. Use a tape recorder if you can.
3. In your head; that is, rehearse mentally, silently reviewing questions and answers.
4. Seated in front of a full-length mirror. You can learn a lot about your body language using this technique.

One important "don't": don't try to memorize your answers. Don't lock yourself into one set of words, one way of telling someone about yourself. Because if you do, you'll come to depend on those words. And if you tighten up during an interview and your mind goes blank for a moment, or if the interviewer asks a question that calls for an answer that's a bit different from the one you memorized, you may panic.

One last point. You can rehearse all you want, and it'll help, but there's no substitute for the real thing. The best way to learn how to interview is to actually do it, to put yourself on the firing line, to be interviewed. With that in mind, try not to take your maiden voyage when the "job of a lifetime" is at stake. Instead, get your feet wet interviewing for jobs that you could take or leave. All it takes is a few interviews to get the kinks out and get a feel for what works and what doesn't.

CHAPTER FIVE

How to Have a Great Interview

Once you're thoroughly prepared you'll probably look forward to the acid test. Unfortunately, there's a fair chance that you'll have to wait just a little bit longer than you'd care to. The cause of this delay is the screening interview.

THE SCREENING INTERVIEW

The first interview with any large company is often a screening interview with someone in the personnel department. Screening interviews usually last about ten minutes and are designed to screen out, in as short a time as possible, applicants who are clearly not qualified for the job. The intent is to find out if something about you is noticeably out of place: for example, if your dress and grooming are sloppy, if you have difficulty relating to others, or if your qualifications are clearly not right for the job.

71

While the screening interview normally doesn't last very long, it is not to be taken lightly. If the interviewer, for whatever reasons, decides he doesn't like you, you're history. So regard the screening interview as a serious first hurdle, and act accordingly.

HOW A JOB INTERVIEW IS STRUCTURED

If you get past the screening interview—and usually you will—you can expect an interview that'll have five parts or phases:

1. Getting started
2. Being asked, and answering, questions about yourself
3. Being told about the job and the company
4. Asking the interviewer questions about the job, the company, and the community
5. Wrapping up and saying good-bye

To help you deal effectively with each of these phases, we're going to review a number of do's and don'ts.

Phase One: Getting Started

"Getting started" includes getting to the interview, arriving with things you might need, greeting the interviewer, and any small talk that might precede questions about yourself. "Getting started," and the way you go about it, helps to create the interviewer's first impression of you. This makes getting started important, since a good first impression will almost always increase the interviewer's interest in you, cause the interviewer to regard you as a more serious candidate, and make him want to know more about you. Unfortunately, a bad first impression usually has the opposite effect, and can take you out of the race before you've gotten out of the gate. So treat this phase seriously, and plan to make it work for you.

How you dress, your body language, and how you speak each have a great deal to do with how well you get through this phase of the interview. Other things that'll help are as follows:

1. Don't bring anyone with you when you go on an interview. If a parent, a brother or sister, or a friend accompanies you, have them wait in the car, take a walk around the block, or go window-shopping. Don't let them come with you to the reception area. It's not professional, and it isn't going to help you.

2. Get there ten minutes before the interview is scheduled to begin, tell the receptionist you're early for your appointment, ask directions to the nearest restroom, and ask him to wait till you return before telling the interviewer that you've arrived. Going to the restroom before an interview will give you a chance to make sure everything is in place: that your hair is combed, your hands and face are clean, there's no lipstick on your teeth, your tie is straight, your shirt's tucked in, and your bladder's empty.

3. Never arrive late for an interview. It doesn't help when you have to begin by apologizing.

4. Bring several copies of your resume, for two reasons:
   • The interviewer may have misplaced his copy, spilled coffee on it, or not have received it.
   • When the interview is over, the interviewer may want you to meet someone else. That someone else probably hasn't heard of you, hasn't seen your resume, and will want to. So have one ready.

5. Bring a pen and paper. You may want to write something down—either during the interview or after it's over.

6. Bring a typed list of the names, titles, business addresses, and phone numbers of three or four people who would recommend you for the job. If you're asked for your references, a typed list will make a much better impression than one which you hurriedly write down or dictate to the interviewer.

7. If you can get a letter praising the work you did else-

where, and if it's at all relevant to the kind of work you'll be doing if you're hired, bring the letter with you and show it to the interviewer when the time seems right. It's one more thing that'll set you apart from the other applicants, and it'll give the interviewer tangible evidence of some of the things you've been saying about yourself.

8. Be poised and confident. You have a lot to offer, and if this company is lucky, you're going to go to work for them.

9. If you smoke, don't light up unless the interviewer does. A lot of people are bothered by cigarette smoke. If the interviewer is one of them and you smoke anyway, you'll create tension. Either he'll ask you to put it out, which won't be comfortable for either of you, or he'll suffer in silence, which will be worse.

10. Don't chew gum. It smacks of adolescence.

Phase Two: Being Asked, and Answering, Questions About Yourself

Never go on an interview without a really good idea of the things you want to tell the interviewer about yourself. Do you want to talk about the kind of person you are, your values, the things that motivate you? Do you want to talk about the particular academic or work experiences that relate to the job? Do you want to talk about why you want to work for this particular company? Arrive prepared to do so.

Normally, you'll be asked questions during the course of the interview that'll give you a chance to say the things you want to about yourself. If you're not, create an opportunity to do so. For example, you might say, "I'd like to tell you a few things about myself that I think will give you a better idea of the kind of person I am and the contribution I could make to this company." Never let an interviewer keep you from telling him why you're special, why you're an outstanding candidate for the job. This kind of statement will give you the chance to do that. It'll also say to the interviewer that you care enough to make the effort.

During the course of every interview, one of the most important things you're going to do is listen. If you don't listen carefully, you're going to hurt yourself. To keep that from happening, keep these do's and don'ts in mind:

1. Don't be distracted by other sights and sounds, things that the interviewer says or does that irritate you, or the interviewer's grammar or accent.

2. Don't plot strategy or formulate replies in your head if it means not listening to the interviewer.

3. If the interviewer says something and you don't know what he means or wants, don't be afraid to say so. For example, you might say, "I don't think I understand what you just said about . . ." Don't let anything that's unclear or confusing go by in the hope that the interviewer will say something else that will clear up the mystery, or that it won't matter. A forthright, polite request for clarification will never be perceived by a reasonable interviewer as a shortcoming.

4. A number of interviewers will begin an interview by asking you to "tell me about yourself." When they do, they're giving you a chance to get off to a flying start. Because it's so general, this question gives you the opportunity to talk about the most outstanding things you've done. These things may have to do with your education, may be job-related, may stem from community involvement. Whatever they are, talk about them. It's one of the best ways you have of letting the interviewer know that you're special.

   Besides talking about the most outstanding things you've done, take the time to talk about your personal life: your family, interests, or favorite sports. They'll give the interviewer a feel for you as a person, and if he likes what he hears, you'll take a big step forward. To make sure that happens, open up just enough to get the conversation going, then put the ball in the interviewer's court. Find out what he likes, then talk about it. Here's an example of how this can work:

APPLICANT: I love sports, both as a player and a fan. How about you?

INTERVIEWER: I've always liked sports, especially tennis. I try to play at least twice a week, and I love to watch the major tournaments.

APPLICANT: Me too. Did you see any of the Wimbledon matches last week?

INTERVIEWER: I managed to catch the women's finals. I thought it was a great match.

APPLICANT: So did I. Both players were really at the top of their games.

By now you get the idea. Find a topic that you're both interested in and get into it. It'll get the interviewer to like you, and that can make him evaluate just about everything else you say more favorably than he otherwise would.

5. When you're asked a question that's going to require a fairly complex reply, try to organize your answer. Suppose you're asked what you look for in a job. You might say there are a number of things, then list them. For example: one, you want a job that interests and challenges you; two, a job that provides you with opportunities to grow; three, a job that enables you to work with and for talented, committed people; and so on.

6. Don't make any claims that you can't support with specific examples or illustrations. For example, don't claim that you like to take charge of situations, that you like to lead, unless you can support that claim with specific instances in which you did in fact take charge or lead.

7. Don't volunteer information about yourself that can hurt your chances: shortcomings, bad habits, courses you failed or jobs you lost. However, if the interviewer does ask a potentially embarrassing question about your educational or job history, don't try to dance around it. Very few people have flawless histories. Some of you

may have done badly in college for a while, getting poor grades. Others may have tried two or three majors before finding one they liked or could live with. Others may have transferred because they were unhappy. Some of you may even have flunked out, then gone back and earned your degrees. Similarly, some of you may have had a hard time on a job. Or may have quit in disgust. Or may have been fired. There's a fair chance that the person who interviews you will ask a question or two about these experiences. If the question comes up, deal with it. Talk about what happened, be ready with a good reason as to why it happened, and if it taught you anything, say so.

8. Don't be dishonest. There's a big difference between telling the interviewer some things about yourself and leaving out others, and telling the interviewer things about yourself that aren't true. Being selective is a reasonable, useful strategy. Lying is not, for several reasons:

- Being honest, particularly about things that can be checked out, is always safer. For example, the company may ask to see your transcript or they may call your references. If you lied and they find out, you're dead in the water.

- If you tell the interviewer that you've got more education, more experience, and/or more skills than you really have and he believes you, you run the risk of being given a job that you won't be able to handle. If that happens, there's a good chance you'll end up hurting yourself.

- You want to be hired for what you are, not for what you can pretend to be. Besides, if you are hired, it'll be easier to be the real you on the job than the fabricated you.

9. Make sure you're understood. If you say something that you think may not be clear or may be misinterpreted, elaborate in a way that leaves no room for doubt.

10. If you don't know the answer to a question, don't be afraid to say so.

11. Don't be afraid to disagree with the interviewer, but be diplomatic if you do.

12. If the interviewer disagrees with something you've said, tactfully stand your ground if you believe in the position you've taken.

13. Don't appear to be desperate for the job. All you'll do is make the interviewer think it's your last hope. If he thinks that, he won't think much of you.

14. If you don't like an interviewer, don't let that stop you from doing your best. The vibrations you'll get from interviewers won't always be good ones. Don't let that stand in your way—unless the interviewer will be the person you report to if you take the job. If he is, pack it in and look elsewhere.

15. Don't look at your watch. Wanting to know the time can say several things to the interviewer, all of them bad:
    • You're thinking about something else.
    • You're worried about whether you'll finish in time to get to another appointment.
    • You're anxious and wish to leave.

    Whatever the interviewer thinks, it won't help. What it will do is disrupt the rapport that's being created. So keep your eyes on the interviewer and away from your watch.

16. Sometimes you may find yourself being interviewed by four or five people at the same time. This is known as a group interview. Group interviews are used to save time. They're also used to get an idea of how well you handle a little pressure. Two features of the group interview can make it hard to handle:
    • These often lack flow or continuity. For example, when you're interviewed by one person, you can expect to be asked several questions about your education, then questions about the jobs you've held, then questions about yourself, and so on. In contrast, the group

interview can jump unpredictably from one topic to the second, then back to the first, then to a third, then back to the second, and so on. Pretty soon, you don't know whether you're coming or going. This can happen because each of the people interviewing you has particular questions he wants answered, and some may not be willing to wait patiently till the topics they're interested in come up. But that's okay, because they can only ask one question at a time, and all the questions are about you—a subject you should know very well and like to talk about.

- The second thing about group interviews that can make them disconcerting is the inclination of some interviewers to ask you a question while you're answering someone else's question. If this happens, politely tell the person who interrupted you that you'll "get to his question in a minute," then finish answering the question you were originally asked.

17. Don't be intimidated by an interviewer's silence. Occasionally an interviewer will test your poise by not speaking after you've replied to a question. He'll just sit there and look at you. Don't lose your composure and blurt out something just to break the silence. Instead, play his game. Look at him and don't say a word. If he doesn't respond by speaking, ask him if there's anything else he'd like to know.

18. Read the interviewer and respond accordingly. Gauge the interviewer's reactions to the things you're saying and the way you're saying them. Does the interviewer look interested? Do his questions and body language say to you that he wants to find out what kind of person you are and how well you fit the requirements of the job? If they do, you're probably doing and saying the right things. If they don't, try to find a way to make the interviewer sit up and take notice. Standard answers to his questions won't do it. Taking the initiative might. Find an opening, or create one, and make the strongest possible case you

can for your candidacy. Speak briefly, forcefully, and with conviction. Your spirit, determination, and confidence may turn an interview that's going nowhere into one that gets you a job.

Phase Three: Being Told About the Job and the Company

Do's and don'ts here are straightforward and small in number:

1. Listen carefully. There are lots of things about the job and the company that you'll want to find out. The interviewer will tell you about many of them, but he's likely to miss at least a few. Those are the ones you'll want to ask about when your turn to ask questions comes.
2. Ordinarily, there'll be several chances for you to ask questions as the interviewer tells you about the job and the company. Take advantage of them and create a dialogue. You'll learn more, and it'll make the interview more interesting for you and the interviewer.
3. Grab any opportunity to display initiative and resourcefulness. For example, if the interviewer's comments suggest to you a way to do the job better or help the company, propose it. It'll mark you as different and special.

Phase Four: Asking the Interviewer About the Job, the Company, and the Community

Do's and don'ts are as follows:

1. Ask clear, precise questions that are easy to understand.
2. If you feel you haven't gotten an acceptable answer to a question you've asked, ask the interviewer to tell you more. And don't settle for generalities. Try to get the

interviewer to be specific. Just be careful not to push too hard. He may have a good reason for not answering.

3. Don't ask for information that the interviewer's already given you. It's either a sign that you weren't listening or that you don't process information very well.

4. Make sure you get answers to all your questions. If you're offered the job, those answers will help you decide whether to take it.

Phase Five: Wrapping up and Saying Good-bye

This phase includes the interviewer's closing remarks, dealing with a job offer if it's made, and farewells by interviewer and applicant. There are several do's and don'ts that you should keep in mind:

1. Never ask the interviewer how you did. You're unlikely to get an honest answer, and you'll probably raise doubts about your poise and confidence.

2. If you're offered the job and you want it, make sure you've met the person you'll report to before you accept. Never take a job without meeting and getting a sense of the person you'll work for. While it's unlikely that this person won't interview you before you're hired, it can happen.

3. If you're offered the job and it's your first interview with the company, don't accept or reject the offer until you've had some time to think about it. Before you accept or reject any offer, you want to carefully evaluate everything you've learned about the job and the company. Unfortunately, the elation you're likely to feel when you're offered the job will make that hard to do. So thank the interviewer for the offer, then tell him you'd like a day or two to make up your mind. You'll be making a request that's reasonable. If the interviewer gives you a hard

time, it should raise serious doubts in your mind about the company as a place to work.

4. Thank the interviewer for taking the time to see you, tell him you've enjoyed talking with him, look into his eyes, smile, shake his hand, and say good-bye.

CHAPTER SIX

Things to Do When the Interview Is Over

After the interview is over and you've had a chance to unwind, there are five things you should do:

1. Reaffirm your interest in the job.
2. Contact your references.
3. Review the interview and evaluate your performance.
4. Expect to be interviewed again if the first interview went well.
5. Prepare to respond to an offer.

Let's look at each of these in some detail.

REAFFIRM YOUR INTEREST IN THE JOB

If you decide you want the job, it can never hurt to reaffirm your interest—if you do it right. The right way is a letter that expresses your interest in the job and indicates why you should be hired. When you write, make sure the company's name, the interviewer's name, and every other word is spelled correctly, that there are no errors in grammar, that you use business-letter form, that there are no smudges or erasures, and that you mail the letter no later than the day after you're interviewed. The following letter should give you a good idea of the elements you'll want your follow-up letters to include:

17 Elm Place
Paramus, NJ 07652
May 10, 1989

Mr. John Warren
Account Supervisor
Kinetechnics, Inc.
678 Third Avenue
New York, NY 10022

Dear Mr. Warren:

I'd like to thank you for meeting with me to discuss the position of Assistant Account Executive. Based on our discussion and on what I've learned about your company, I feel that it's a job I want very much and one I could do very well.

As I understand it, you want someone who can become part of a team, learn quickly, handle several assignments at the same time, and work well with clients. I think the things I've done—operating the Used Book Exchange with a small number of students, taking 20 hours of coursework in each of several semesters, and taking courses in which I had to learn quickly or fall behind—indicate that I'm well prepared for the job. More-over, it's a job that I feel will challenge me, provide me with opportunities to contribute and grow, and enable me to work with people who are talented and who care about the work they do.

I look forward to hearing from you.

Sincerely,
Linda James

Let's take a closer look at this letter:

The Interviewer's Name and Address

Use "Mr." if the interviewer is a man. Use "Ms."—not "Miss" or "Mrs."—if the interviewer is a woman. Why? Because you may mistakenly call a "Mrs." a "Miss," or vice versa. Even if you don't, the interviewer may feel that her marital status has nothing to do with her job, and may prefer "Ms."

The interviewer's title should follow his name. If you're not sure what it is or don't know it, don't guess. Just leave it out. It won't make the difference between an offer and a rejection.

Spell the company's name exactly the way the company does; for example, if they use Williams & Co., you should, too. The only abbreviation in the address should be the state. Use U.S. Postal Service designations: for example, NY, FL, and CA.

When you greet the interviewer in your letter, use the interviewer's last name. The interviewer isn't your friend, and this isn't a personal letter.

The Body of the Letter

The body of the letter should be brief, clearly written, and to the point. Use a few short paragraphs, never one long one; they're easier to read and they look better.

Begin by thanking the interviewer for seeing you. Then reaffirm your interest in the job, and tell the interviewer why he should hire you. Do that by briefly summarizing the things you've done that qualify you for the job and your reasons for wanting it. Close by telling him that you look forward to his decision.

The Complimentary Close

"Sincerely" and "Yours truly" are both appropriate.

CONTACT YOUR REFERENCES

If the interviewer has asked for the names of your references, get in touch with them as soon as you can. Tell them that you've just interviewed for a job. Tell them about the job, what it requires, and the name of the company that's trying to fill it. Give them a feel for what you and the interviewer talked about. Tell them that you've given their names as references and that you feel there's a fair chance they'll be called. If they are, tell them you'd appreciate knowing about it as soon as it happens. If it does happen, try to find out what questions the interviewer asked and what answers your references gave. It'll give you a better sense of how you stand, and it'll tell you just how good a reference each of these people really is.

REVIEW THE INTERVIEW AND EVALUATE YOUR PERFORMANCE

Think about the interview and evaluate your performance. If the interview didn't go well, don't let it shake your confidence in yourself. Instead, learn from it.

There are two basic reasons for an interview not going well: the interviewer and the applicant. Let's look at the interviewer first. If you go on enough interviews, you'll probably run into interviewers that you don't like. They might ask dumb questions, they might be vague, they might spend most of the interview talking rather than encouraging you to talk, they might be overly aggressive, they might be rude. And it won't be because of anything you did or didn't do. It's simply because that's the way they are. They're not good interviewers and, as interviewers, they hurt your chances and they hurt their companies. Unfortunately, about all you can do is chalk it up as a bad experience and put it behind you.

If the interview didn't go well because of things you did, brood if you want to but learn from your mistakes. Think about what you did wrong and figure out ways to change, to make it right. Then practice.

Even when an interview goes well, learn from it. First, think about what you did that made it go well, then make sure these things become permanent features of your presentation. Second, examine your performance in an attempt to find ways, even small ones, to make it better.

EXPECT TO BE INTERVIEWED AGAIN IF THE FIRST INTERVIEW WENT WELL

Many companies don't hire anyone, even for entry-level positions, until they've been interviewed and okayed by several people. So if you've only been interviewed once, don't be surprised if you're invited back for a second round. If you are asked to return, go, even if you have doubts about the wisdom of working for the company. A second round of interviews will give you a chance to meet more people and find out more about the company. The more you learn, the better equipped you'll be to make a decision if an offer is made.

PREPARE TO RESPOND TO AN OFFER

Get ready to respond to an offer if it's made. Carefully review the things you've learned about the job, the company, and the community. Think about each of the people you met and the things they said. Then ask yourself if you're interested in doing the kind of work this job requires; if you're likely to acquire new skills and sharpen old ones on this job; if there are opportunities for promotion; if the person you'll report to seems fair, decent, and capable; if you're satisfied with the pay; and if the company seems like a good one. Then decide what your answer will be if they want you.

CHAPTER SEVEN

Until It Happens: Some Last Words

Each interview you have is not just a chance to compete for a job, but a chance to learn, to strengthen and fine-tune important skills. As you interview for different jobs, you'll have the chance to make changes in the way you present yourself, to learn to read interviewers and respond accordingly, to become adept at asking and answering questions, and to discover what works and what doesn't. In important ways, interviewing is like going to school. So prepare for each interview and learn from it, till one of them lands you a job you want.

BIBLIOGRAPHY

Advertising Age. Chicago: Crain Communications, weekly.

Adweek. New York: A/S/M Communications, weekly.

American Hospital Association Guide to the Health Care Field. Chicago: American Hospital Association, annual.

Business Week. New York: McGraw-Hill, weekly.

Career Employment Opportunities Directory (2nd edition). Santa Monica, CA: Ready Reference Press, 1985.

Education Directory: Colleges and Universities. Washington, D.C.: U.S. Department of Education, annual.

Education Directory: Public School Systems. Washington, D.C.: U.S. Department of Education, annual.

Education Directory: State Education Agency Officials. Washington, D.C.: U.S. Department of Education, annual.

Encyclopedia of Associations. Detroit: Gale Research Company, annual.

The Encyclopedia of Careers and Vocational Guidance (7th edition). Chicago: J. G. Ferguson Publishing Company, 1987.

Literary Market Place. New York: R. R. Bowker Company, 1988.

Marketing News. Chicago: American Marketing Association, biweekly.

Million Dollar Directory: America's Leading Public & Private Companies. Parsippany, New Jersey: Dun's Marketing Services, annual.

Moody's Industrial Manual. New York: Moody's Investors Service, annual.

The National Directory for the Performing Arts and Civic Centers (3rd edition). New York: John Wiley & Sons, 1978.

National Directory of Private Social Agencies. Queens Village, NY: Social Service Publications, annual.

The National Job Bank: A Comprehensive Guide to Major Employers in the Nation's Key Job Markets (4th edition). Brighton, MA: Bob Adams, Inc., 1987.

The New York Times. New York: The New York Times Company, daily.

Occupational Outlook Handbook. Washington, D.C.: U.S. Department of Labor, annual.

Places Rated Almanac (2nd edition), by Rick Boyer and David Savageau. Chicago: Rand McNally, 1985.

Publishers Weekly. Marion, Ohio: Bowker Magazine Group, Cahners Magazine Division, weekly.

Standard Directory of Advertisers. Wilmette, IL: National Register Publishing Company, annual.

Standard Rate and Data Business Publication Directory. Wilmette, IL: Standard Rate & Data Service, monthly.

The Wall Street Journal. New York: Dow Jones & Company, daily.

Women's Wear Daily. New York: Fairchild Publications, daily.

The Working Press of the Nation. Chicago: National Research Bureau, annual.